Rolling Harvey down the Hill

by Jack Prelutsky · **illustrated by Victoria Chess**

Greenwillow Books, New York

For Marty Wallach,
who liked the title

 Published by Greenwillow Books, a division of William Morrow & Company, Inc., 1350 Avenue of the Americas, New York, NY 10019. Printed in the United States of America. First Edition   15 14 13 12 11 10 9 8 7 6

Library of Congress Cataloging in Publication Data   Prelutsky, Jack. Rolling Harvey down the hill.   Summary: A collection of humorous poems about the narrator's four friends, one of whom is the obnoxious Harvey. 1. Children's poetry, American. [1. Friendship–Poetry. 2. Humorous poetry. 3. American poetry]   I. Chess, Victoria.   II. Title. PS3566.R36R6   811'.5'4   79-18236   ISBN 0-688-80258-3 ISBN 0-688-84258-5 lib. bdg.

Contents

My Four Friends

I live in an apartment house
next to a vacant lot,
my buddies live there also,
the four best friends I've got.

There's Tony and there's Lumpy
and there's Harvey and there's Will,
and we all hang out together
in the middle of our hill.

Tony's always cheerful,
I think he's really neat
although he wears thick glasses
and is clumsy on his feet.

Lumpy causes trouble,
he's the terror of the block,
he gets away with plenty
'cause he's just too small to sock.

Harvey's mean and nasty,
he's selfish as a pig,
but no one ever hits him
'cause Harvey's just too big.

Will is sort of special,
he acts like a chimpanzee,
I like Will an awful lot
'cause Will's a lot like me.

6

Sometimes
we have races,
and sometimes
we play ball,
but mostly
we're just buddies
doing nothing
much at all.

7

Harvey Always Wins

Every game that Harvey plays,
Harvey always wins,
everybody knows he will
before the game begins.

Follow the leader, leapfrog, tag,
whatever game we choose,
as long as Harvey's in the game
then Harvey doesn't lose.

We hate to play with Harvey,
he loves to spoil our fun,
as soon as a game is over
he shouts, "You see, I won."

Harvey's always showing off,
he wins when he competes,
it isn't that he's better,
it's that Harvey always cheats.

Smoking in the Cellar

I swiped my grandma's cigarettes,
I didn't dare to tell her,
then Lumpy, Tony, Will and me
snuck down into the cellar.

We slipped inside the storage room
and bolted shut the latch.
I gave us each a cigarette
and Tony struck a match.

We lit them up together
and boldly took a puff.
We found out very quickly
that one would be enough.

We coughed and wheezed and sputtered
as we breathed in clouds of smoke,
Will turned white, and Lumpy green,
and Tony and I just choked.

I never want to smoke again
'cause smoking's really dumb.
Next time I feel like smoking,
I think I'll just chew gum.

Willie ate a worm today,
a squiggly, wiggly worm.
He picked it up
from the dust and dirt
and wiped it off
on his brand-new shirt.
Then slurp, slupp
he ate it up,
yes Willie ate a worm today,
a squiggly, wiggly worm.

Willie ate a worm today,
he didn't bother to chew,
and we all stared
and we all squirmed
when Willie swallowed
down that worm.
Then slupp, slurp
Willie burped,
yes Willie ate a worm today,
I think I'll eat one too.

The Race

Harvey think's he's something,
most of the time he's bragging,
his mouth is always open
and his tongue is always wagging.

"I'm smarter than you," brags Harvey,
"I'm bigger and stronger too,
in fact there isn't anything
I can't do better than you."

"Let's race around the block," he said,
giving us all a grin,
"I'll bet you a million dollars
that I'm the one who'll win."

And so we all raced Harvey,
and soon he was ahead
until he turned around to see
by just how much he led.

He tripped and lost his footing
and smacked right into a wall–
it'll be a week till Harvey brags
or plays with us at all.

13

Mr. Mulligan's Window

We broke Mister Mulligan's window
when Anthony hit that home run.
We were warned that we never should play there,
but now it's too late, for it's done.

Oh, we broke Mister Mulligan's window
though nobody wanted to do it,
but as the ball sailed past the outfield,
every last one of us knew it.

It smashed into thousands of pieces
that shattered all over the place,
and out of the house he came charging
with a terrible look on his face.

He screamed as we ran down the sidewalk,
and I ran the fastest of all.
Though Anthony busted the window,
I had written MY name on the ball.

The Fight

I got mad at Willie
and called him a dirty name,
Willie punched me in the jaw
and so I did the same.

Then we grabbed each other
and we spun each other 'round,
we socked and kicked and wrestled
and we tussled on the ground.

The fight was very even,
we're about the exact same size,
Willie bloodied up my nose
and I blacked both his eyes.

Back and forth we struggled,
and forth and back we hit,
our mothers finally broke us up
and so we had to quit.

Willie and I were pals again
as soon as the fight was done,
neither of us lost the fight,
but neither of us won.

Nobody Calls Him Jim

James lives in our neighborhood
but nobody calls him Jim,
he isn't very friendly
so we never play with him.

He goes and does his homework
as soon as he gets home,
his shoes are always polished
and his hair is always combed.

He always wears a bow tie
and he's awfully polite,
he asks "please" and answers "thank you"
and he doesn't like to fight.

I've heard he eats his vegetables
without the slightest fuss,
and he even asks for seconds–
no he's not the same as us.

I think there must be something
terribly wrong with him,
James lives in our neighborhood
but nobody calls him Jim.

Lumpy Is My Friend

Lumpy likes to pick his nose,
then wipe his fingers on my clothes.
It doesn't matter, I suppose,
for Lumpy is my friend.

He hides my shoes, he steals my hats,
he pulls the tails of dogs and cats,
oh, Lumpy is the brat of brats,
still, Lumpy is my friend.

Lumpy thinks it's lots of fun
to shoot me with his water gun
and trip me when I try to run,
still, Lumpy is my friend.

He stuffs my pockets full of rice
and down my back slips chunks of ice,
I know that Lumpy isn't nice,
but Lumpy is my friend.

Harvey is a tub of lard,
munching candy in the yard,
and should we ask for just a bit,
he quickly gobbles all of it.

When Harvey has some spare dessert,
he hides it from us in his shirt,
and never shares his ice cream cone;
he says, "It's mine, go get your own."

But when he sees us chewing gum,
he yells, "How come I can't have some?"
Harvey is a tub of lard,
munching candy in the yard.

No Girls Allowed

When we're playing tag
and the girls want to play,
we yell and we scream
and we chase them away.

When we're playing stickball
or racing our toys
and the girls ask to join,
we say, "Only for boys."

We play hide-and-go-seek
and the girls wander near.
They say, "Please let us hide."
We pretend not to hear.

We don't care for girls
so we don't let them in,
we think that they're dumb–
and besides, they might win.

The Practical Joke

Harvey likes to practice knots
with different kinds of string.
He bragged to me and Willie
he could tie up anything.

"Let me try my knots on you,"
he asked us both one day.
Willie wanted to show him up
and so we said OK.

Harvey took some clothesline
and he tied us both to trees,
he wound it round our shoulders
and made knots behind our knees.

He tied us very carefully
with lots and lots of rope.
"Can you get loose?" he asked us,
and Willie answered, "Nope!"

"You're positive you can't get free?"
I said, "We're tied too tight."
Then Harvey grinned and smugly said,
"I guess I did it right."

Harvey pinched and tickled us,
we yelled, "That isn't fair!"
He laughed and pulled our trousers down
and left us standing there.

25

Tony and the Quarter

Tony's my neighbor
and Tony's my friend.
Today Tony's ma
gave him money to spend.

He slapped my behind
and he said with a laugh,
"Whatever I get,
you can have almost half.

I got a whole quarter,
I'll split it with you.
Let's go get some candy
and bubble gum too."

So happily downhill
the two of us tore,
to see what a quarter
would buy at the store.

But things didn't work
just the way that we planned,
Tony tripped—and the quarter
flew out of his hand.

It rolled down the sidewalk
and oh, what a pain!
We couldn't catch up
and it went down the drain.

Such a dumb thing to do,
oh, it made me so sore.
Still, I guess I like Tony
as much as before.

Lumpy Chases Pigeons

Lumpy chases pigeons,
he shoos them down the street,
he likes to see them scamper
on their little pigeon feet.

Whenever Lumpy spots them,
he hollers "Scat!" and "Scoot!"
They run away in terror
with Lumpy in pursuit.

The rest of us like pigeons
and toss them crusts of bread,
but Lumpy never feeds them,
he chases them instead.

Lumpy yells at pigeons,
"I'll get you birds I bet."
In all his years of trying
he's never caught one yet.

As soon as they hear Lumpy,
down the block they go,
the pigeon flock moves swiftly
and Lumpy's very slow.

Rolling Harvey down the Hill

Harvey whimpers, Harvey whines
and Harvey is a pest,
Harvey tells us every day
that Harvey is the best.
Harvey's always butting in,
his mouth is never still,
so Tony, Lumpy, Will and me
rolled Harvey down the hill.

See him rolling, rolling, rolling,
see him rolling down the hill.
All the way from top to bottom
we rolled Harvey down the hill.

29

Harvey never shares with us,
he always wants his way,
Harvey lies and Harvey cheats
at every game we play.
Harvey pulls too many pranks,
we finally had our fill,
so Tony, Lumpy, Will and me
rolled Harvey down the hill.

   See him rolling, rolling, rolling,
   see him rolling down the hill.
   All the way from top to bottom
   we rolled Harvey down the hill.

Harvey is a bossy guy,
he likes to pick a fight,
Harvey thinks he's never wrong
and no one else is right.
Today we paid back Harvey,
Tony, Lumpy, me and Will,
when we knocked him to the sidewalk
and rolled Harvey down the hill.

   See him rolling, rolling, rolling,
   see him rolling down the hill.
   All the way from top to bottom
   we rolled Harvey down the hill.

Once we'd started Harvey rolling,
Harvey couldn't stop.
We ran beside him, laughing
as we watched him go kerplop.
Over and over Harvey tumbled,
and he tumbled down until
Harvey reached the very bottom
and stopped rolling down the hill.

See him rolling, rolling, rolling,
see him rolling down the hill.
All the way from top to bottom
we rolled Harvey down the hill.

Jack Prelutsky

was born and raised in New York City but now makes his home in Seattle, Washington. He has been entertaining young readers for years with his funny and original books of poems, including *The Queen of Eene,* illustrated by Victoria Chess; *The Snopp on the Sidewalk;* and *Nightmares,* a chilling collection of monster poems; all ALA Notable Books.

Victoria Chess

was born in Chicago, attended school in Providence, Rhode Island, and Switzerland, and studied art at the Boston Museum School. She is the author-artist of *Alfred's Alphabet Walk* and the co-author, with Edward Gorey, of *Fletcher and Zenobia.* She has also illustrated many popular books, including *A Ship in a Storm on the Way to Tarshish* by Norma Farber.